Guns Across America

Prologue

Guns across America has been the calling of this great nation since our beginning when America was discovered. Our nation had many struggles that required the use of guns. The wilderness was full of wild animals and savages as it is reported in history. To survive, the pilgrims had to use guns. It was a common thing for men or women to carry a gun and keep guns in their homes. This was the start of our great nation and through our history, things never changed. **Guns across America** continues.

We need to make drastic changes as a nation as we no longer need to fear wild animals or savages in our communities. The only savages it seems today are those who already live in our society among us as normal human beings. But let's look at how our nation is growing and has become great with the use of guns. Then let us look at society today, and how guns affect all of us. It is true: we must be able to use a gun for hunting and even to protect our homes. The question now is what type of guns are necessary.

Pilgrim Gun

Modern Day Gun

1

Shirley Smith-Lopez (Author)

Author's Biography

My name is Shirley Smith-Lopez. I was born to a humble family in the hills of Kentucky. At the tender age of five years I moved to Mansfield, Ohio where I received my formal education and grew up with the knowledge that someday, I would become a writer. At the tender age of ten, I wrote articles for Reader's Digest and a popular song that is still sung today in the field of country music.

I graduated from the *Ohio State University* while still living in Ohio and became a Certified Public Accountant. I worked for years with **Five Cousins** and then with the **Mansfield Board of Education.** Both my parents and my only brother passed away leaving me to be alone but not lonely.

I met and married my husband and moved to Holland, Michigan. While living in Holland, I attended *Davenport University and Hope College*. I got my degree in Business Administration along with one in Computer Science. I further took classes in *theology* and became an ordained minister. I decided that I did not want to be a minister over any denomination, so I decided to help as many as I could by being non-denominational.

I adopted four children that my husband had in his previous marriage as their mother had passed, and I wanted very much to care and love them. I also had one son, **Michael**, who married **Karen Jenks** and blessed me with two daughters. The girls **Abigail and Chole** have become the *light of my life*. But notwithstanding, my oldest daughter blessed me with two children as well. Kathryn Jones has a son **Victor** who I am very proud of with all his achievements in life and successes.

She also has a daughter **Jessica** who is very beautiful and blessed me with two great-granddaughters, **Mia and Harper**. My other daughter **Cynthia Eastman** is a beautiful red head, and she bore four children whom I am proud to say are handsome and beautiful as well.

The oldest daughter, **Chanel**, lives in the south and is very talented. She is a beautiful addition to our family. The youngest daughter, **Cecilia**, is a beauty queen and blessed me with a great-granddaughter, **Luna Marie**.

The youngest son **Jacob** and **Vinnie,** his wife, is now expecting a baby soon, and we are very happy for this welcome addition to the family. **Jacob** is a very talented artist and hopes to someday become an architect.

Cindy's oldest son, **Anthony**, blessed the family with his son *Colton* and daughter *Addy*. His wife **Sarah** is expecting again soon, and we are very much happy for this new arrival. **Colton**, my only great grandson, is a real fighter. At the age of three, he was found to have cancer in his eye, and it had to be removed. *He is a fighter and a winner!*

I lived many years in Holland, Michigan raising my family among the tulips enjoying the parade and the quaint little town along the lakeshore. Not only is Holland famous for its **Tulip Time Parade**, but it also has a beautiful beach along *Lake Michigan.*

My husband Fermin, who is many years older than I, is a true soldier in himself. He worked for *forty-seven years* at **H.J. Heinz USA** before he retired. He now has suffered from open heart surgery and multiple strokes. His family loves him very much, and he has shown that he is a **real fighter** for his family and his own life.

Our other son, **Ken**, recently married **Jodi**, and they live very happily in Saugatuck, Michigan. He is dedicated to his work and very athletic. The oldest son **Fermin Jr**. is an artist and remains a recluse.

I am presently living in Lansing, Michigan with my husband and writing my books and still doing some freelance work for others. I worked many years for **Sam's Club** in the marketing department. I enjoy writing, reading, taking long walks, riding bicycles, and helping others. I am also working as a volunteer for the **Homeless Angels**, started by **Mike Karl** to help those on the streets to find haven, providing food, clothes, and getting them jobs. Mr. Karl is a wonderful individual who has a great love for everyone.

In my life, I have met many people and very few that I did not find anything good in their lives. You can find good in just about everyone's life if you only look for it. But first you must put good things in your own life. This is my family whom I am very proud.

In conclusion, we hope that you enjoy reading my books and find that some are a benefit to your health and healing. God bless and thank all of you for buying my books and supporting me.

Michael Lopez- Cynthia Eastman-Christina- Kathryn Jones- Fermin (Aaron) and-Ken Lopez

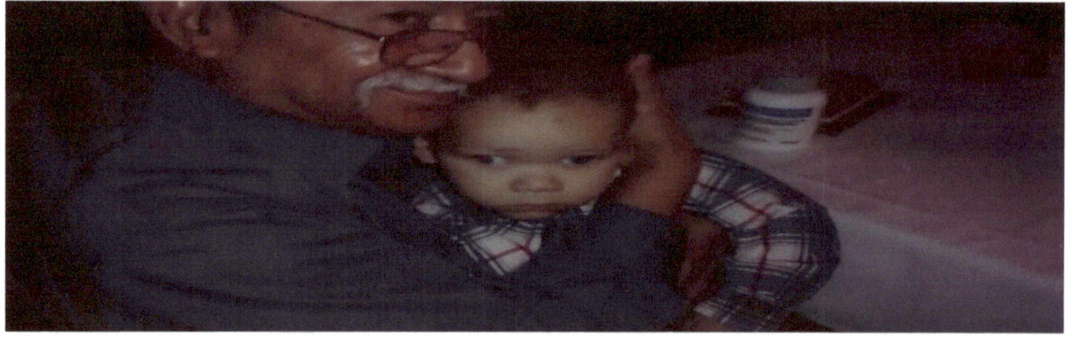

Grandpa Fermin & Great-Grandson Colton

Grandma Shirley & Chloe and Abby

Mia and Harper Cushing (Kathy Jones Granddaughter's)

Contents:

In the early days, people who settled this new world needed to have a gun to survive. The gun was important to provide the family with meat for the table, protect the family from wild beasts, and from the Indians. Pilgrim families feared for their life because of all the dangers that they needed to face.

As American lives moved forward, towns were formed, and people moved to cities. It was not always necessary to carry a gun unless you were going hunting or about to come to town. There was still plenty of wild animals around, which was cause for concern. Families had to make sure that they had a rifle or a pistol to be safe. In some areas, snakes were still abundant and dangerous, which meant that pistols were in great demand.

Then as things became more civilized, it became apparent that the era of the **"Wild West"** was formed and many men and some women wore guns on their side. It was common to have gun fights and killings kept growing. The towns hired sheriffs, but that was not always a successful as the people liked it to be. Bank robberies would happen causing guards to carry guns. Pony Express carried the mail, but the riders had to have guns for their protection. When they left the city limits, it would be necessary to carry a gun for their protection.

The first war was that amongst the people of this new world and Great Britain. We were able to gain our freedom and run out any foreign entity. Our first line of defense was **"Minute Men"** who were the local farmers and merchants. When they saw the British soldiers coming, they would grab their guns and be prepared in a minute's notice. That is where the title comes from **"Minute Men."**

Minute Men Always Ready

Continental Army vs Great Britain

George Washington was the first Commander of the American forces and his troops were known as the Continental Army. He was a very smart commander and knew how to defeat the British making us a free nation. Guns had to be used, and they were whatever the men could muster up. So many men had rifles some had pistols while others just used knives. We became what is now known as the United States of America. Our progress was inevitable because there were many who wanted to move forward. We had no gun laws that were universal instead the laws were made up by the town or district that people lived in.

In some major cities you had to check your gun with the local sheriff before you could get into town. In some places you could wear it and use it at will. There was much lawlessness especially out west. America grew, and people survived, and guns existed. No one questioned a man with a gun! There were many Indian wars, which required the keeping of guns during this era as well. Family feuds existed over property and when the gold rush days started again, guns settled the problems. **Guns Across America** was a common thing to keep peace, provide food, and provide protection for families.

When the Civil War broke out, there was again a call for the use of guns. Many men and women fought for the cause of freedom and took up arms. The guns were ever popular and in just about all homes. President Lincoln was finally able to get folks to lay down their guns and unite. People were so tired of the killings and ready for peace. There were other battles during this time. The Battle of the Alamo for instance where the Mexicans fought and took the Alamo from the Texans. But they retreated across the border and Texas remained a part of the United States.

Theodore Roosevelt also had a battle with Cuba and won, but we did not claim that country. Coal miners also had battles between them and the mine owners, which caused the loss of life. There were many little incidents that occurred too numerous to mention, but guns were always being used. Early America used guns to grow and survive, or we would not exist like we do today. **Guns Across America** has always been visible and in use for the survival of this nation and the growth that we see today.

The National Rifle Association commonly known as the NRA has been in existence since November 16, 1871. The founder George Wood Wingate believed in freedom first and the focus of the organization today is the right to bear arms for all Americans. Its corporate office is in Fairfax, Virginia.

The **National Rifle Association of America (NRA)** is an American nonprofit organization that advocates for gun rights.[5][6][7]

Founded in 1871, the group has informed its members about firearm-related bills since 1934, and it has directly lobbied for and against legislation since 1975.[8] It has been called the oldest continuously operating civil rights organization and the "largest and best-funded lobbying organization in the United States".[9]

Founded to advance rifle marksmanship, the modern NRA continues to teach firearm competency and safety. The organization also publishes several magazines and sponsors competitive marksmanship events.[8] Membership surpassed 5 million in May 2013.[5]

Observers and lawmakers see the NRA as one of the top three most influential lobbying groups in Washington, D.C.[10][11] The NRA Institute for Legislative Action (NRA-ILA) is its lobbying arm, which manages its political action committee, the Political Victory Fund (PVF). Over its history the organization has influenced legislation, participated in or initiated lawsuits, and endorsed or opposed various candidates.

The NRA has been criticized by gun control and gun rights advocacy groups, political commentators, and politicians.[12][13] The NRA's oldest organized critics include the gun control advocacy groups the Brady Campaign, the Coalition to Stop Gun Violence (CSGV), and the Violence Policy Center (VPC). Twenty-first century groups include Every town for Gun Safety (formerly Mayors Against Illegal Guns), Moms Demand Action, and Americans for Responsible Solutions. The organization has been the focus of intense criticism in the aftermath of high-profile shootings, such as the Sandy Hook Elementary School shooting and the Stoneman Douglas High School shooting.

From Wikipedia, the free encyclopedia

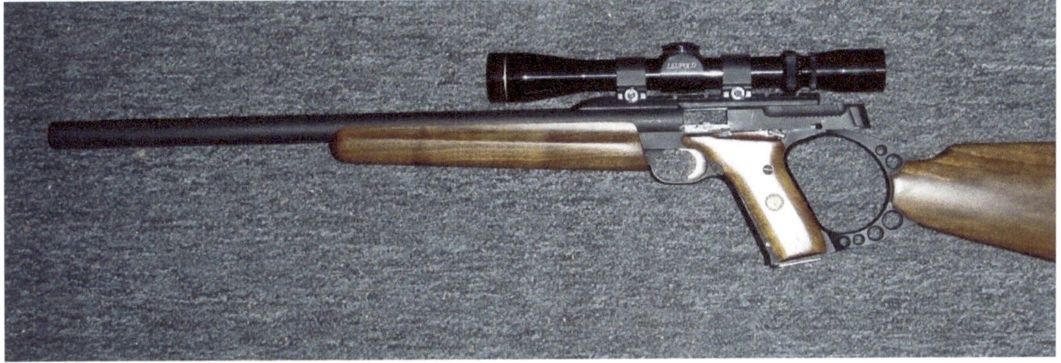

Rifles kill people in the hands of the wrong people

Be a Responsible Gun Owner!

Do We Need Guns Today?

Save the Children!!

Today, righteously so, many folks are very upset about school shootings. It is one of the most horrible events in our modern society. However, the truth be told, we have been plagued by these types of massacres all throughout the centuries. The fact is that earlier massacres were done to the Indians after the Civil War. The army then turned its attention towards driving the Indians farther out of the country and at times whole villages of Indians were slaughtered.

Early American Indian village

We speak about how badly Geronimo was when it came to killing the white man, but he started on his killing spree after our military had raided his village killing his wife and sons. The American Indian fought back in the best way they knew how and that was with a vengeance. Imagine if you would be coming home after shopping for food and finding everyone on your street gunned down, slaughtered if you please. You find your whole family killed right before your eyes and your neighbors.

The Calvary of early American soldiers

In a sense that is what happened to Geronimo and his men when they returned from hunting foo. They found that the people in the village had been massacred without mercy. No survivors! There were no politicians to go to or government officials to take their problems to. It was up to the Indian to resolve the problem. They took several steps by moving their family farther west, so they were able to save them. Then it was time to stop the white man and kill those who showed their people no mercy. That is just the way that it was back in early America. Guns ruled the west! The west ruled with guns!

The Apache Indian was not the only tribes that rebelled. Many others did the same. The Sioux for instance were faced with the extinction of the buffalo. The white man killed the animals to make way for the railroads. The buffalo was the Indian's source of meat and their skin made clothes. All along the way, the Indian was massacred for territory, wealth, and just because they were an Indian. This was a heartless time for people because the Indians did their fair share of killing as well. The war raged on and both sides were killed by guns, knives, swords, and tomahawks. **Guns across America** were prevalent. People lived and died by the gun.

Guns were often used during this time!

The era of the gun being over in the wild west only changed up to the era of the gun in modern civilization with the Prohibition, a law that prevented the sale of alcohol in the United States. This was a time in our history that we could not be proud of because of the crimes committed. Prohibition was in every state and every state was in confusion. For instance, Chicago had bred some of the worst gangsters that not only sold booze but would also use a gun to kill their opponent. Chicago, Illinois laid fame to such men as Al Capone, Dutch Schultz, and other notorious men who killed daily. It was nothing unusual to find dead bodies in the east river.

Other areas had the same problems with gangsters in New York, Pennsylvania, Wisconsin, and as far west as California. It seemed everyone wanted to make money by selling booze, and everyone carried a gun. The massacres continued with the "Valentine's Day" shooting and other shootings. It was not only the killings in Chicago, but all over this nation people were being shot. One did not have to be a gangster at that time to get into the line of fire.

When World War II broke out this nation was not prepared with weapons such as guns. President Roosevelt called on the gangsters of our nations to donate their guns as our first line of defense. It was said that thousands of guns of all types ended up on the docks to help in our defense. If it had not been for the stock pile of guns, we would not have been able to arm our soldiers. Guns played an important part in our nation's defense. The laws that existed did not affect those who had guns as the president forgave anyone who donated his/her gun for our defense.

Other parts of the nation also wanted to bear arms, and they did for a very long time. It is true that in the south, many men made moonshine and other drinks but needed their guns to protect the steels. The government would chase them down but to no end. These moonshiners would get into battles with each other and there would be shootouts killing many on both sides. The southern people also tended to get into feuds killing off each other with the use of guns. **Guns across America** has been prevalent ever since the founding of this great nation.

Coal miners' strike against mine owners

Guns were used by the coal miners to protect their interests against the mining companies. The battle raged on with strikes and guns being used. The mine owners would send in strike breakers, and the miners would bring out the guns and the war raged on. The same thing was happening out west with the railroads. It was hard to get the railroad through some areas, so the bosses had to arm the workers. They had to fight off Indians and people in towns who objected. In Missouri for instance the railroad owners took the farms away from the people. The people fought back by robbing them and robbing the banks. Men like Jessie James and Cole Younger took up arms to defend their family and to take back what was rightfully theirs.

All through our history, we are noted for winning wars and conquering territories using the gun. It is not secret that many people used their guns in this wild frontier to defend home and family. Unfortunately, there were those who used guns to commit crimes as well. Guns are very dangerous in the wrong hands. People have been killed by accident by someone who picked up a gun and did not know how to use it. Children have shot children by finding a loaded gun and playing with it. The use of a gun should not be taken lightly. It is a serious business to own a gun and the gun owner needs to know how to handle the gun and keep those around him safe.

"The Right to Bear Arms" has become a thorn in American society today. It was an essential law in our history to tame this country and make it safe for us to live in. Today, it is not essential to have a gun. We are not supposed to have to walk down the streets with a gun strapped on our side. We should not have to worry about getting our family off to work and school because someone with a gun is waiting around the corner to shoot them.

The NRA and gun clubs across America fight to protect those who want to have a gun, but we need to form a group to fight to protect us against those who have a gun and are not responsible to own it. It is true there are thousands of people in America today who like to go hunting and/or like to shoot guns at targets for fun. Many people just like to collect guns. Let me say on their behalf many of them are responsible people who would not think of hurting anyone much less shooting a child. This is a well-earned privilege by many who have served in the military to protect us from harm.

These folks should be able to buy a gun or guns and use them for hunting, target practice, and collection. This situation is very difficult because no one wants to take away the rights of responsible adults. Unfortunately, there are those who own a gun that are not responsible adults. They may be careless with the handling of guns causing accidents that are fatal to family members. The gun owner should always make sure the gun is put up in a safe place and is not loaded. The gun needs to be put into a locked case along with the bullets. Safety first is always a must for the gun owner.

It takes more than just telling someone to be safe and keep your gun locked up. Instead, new laws and rules need to be put into place for the gun owner. "The Right to Bear Arms" law is no longer sufficient it needs to be ratified and specific rules added. A good gun owner wants to keep his/her gun in a safe manner and honestly does not mind rules of safety. In most cases, the rules behind being safe are already being done by the gun owner. It is those who are not responsible who usually fight any change. We have lost enough children and adults by mad gunmen. People who get access to guns and who are mentally disturbed are the cause of most shootings. It those people who should not have a gun in their possession.

Chapter 6 – The Bill of Rights

The Bill of Rights states the following:

Amendment 11 A well-regulated militia, being necessary to the security of a free state, the right of the people to keep and bear arms, shall not be infringed. Amendment 11. Let us look at this Amendment more closely and see how it was intended when written and how it is affecting us now.

A well-regulated militia, being necessary to the security of a free state was needed when this document was written. Remember the minute men were just regular farmers who lived in the country and had to be able to grab their gun in less than a minute to protect home, family, and country from foreign invaders.

The right of the people to keep and bear arms shall not be infringed upon. This was a necessary law because not only did people in that time need to protect family against foreign invaders, but it was needed to shoot game for food, protect against wild animals, and other earth shattering experiences.

That is the reason the law was written back in the start of this great nation. Today, we have a fully trained army, and we do not have to use a weapon for protection, to feed our family, or protect our home. Today we have a National Guard that works within the country to help us and protect us from harm's way.

This is not a law of convenience. It is a law that needs changed to fit our society today. The law is so obsolete that it is not funny! It does not cover anything pertaining to our society today. It should read the right to own a weapon to go hunting or to collect it. The ability to be a responsible gun owner is required as well as the passing of a psychiatric exam. We must pass a physical exam lots of times to do certain functions like participate in sports or be in the military. The right to own a gun should require an exam that will give the owner a clean mental bill of health.

Let us never again fear that our children will be killed by someone who is mentally unstable and uses a gun to get what they think is right or just to be able to say that they were a shooter who killed multiple people. It is not being responsible that our government allows this to happen.

Guns Across America affect many people in our nation no matter what their race. It is unfortunate but true. People are often picked out just because of their race. At a comedy club, I heard a black comedian say that **"Black Men"** are considered an endangered species. That is not true he replied because we protect our endangered species but not the **"Black Man."** Across our nation young black men are harassed, imprisoned, and killed not because of committing a crime but because of their race.

This is not only happening to the colored race but also to Hispanics, Asians, and other races depending on where they live. Children of mixed races have it even harder, which should not be happening. The ability to get a gun is just too easy, and in the hands of the wrong people, it can be a disaster. There are groups of people whose deliberate purpose is the destruction of people of color, religion, or political viewpoints. We in America today need to take heed and stamp these types of organizations. It is not good that they can get their hands on military type of weapons.

The purpose of these types of weapons is to be used by the military to protect us on foreign shores. Those who have access to them here, should be in the military, police department, or National Guard. It is needed when groups attack our facilities, rob major places, or sometimes when prisoners riot. It is not for sport or hunting animals as in this country we do not have animals that large and most hunters can use a better type of gun for hunting.

Then we need to better train our police and those who are there to protect us, so that they do not use the weapons against us. It is not always wise to just give any man or woman a gun and appoint them as service men in uniform as police etc. There have been many people who were killed by armed police. Unfortunately, prejudice is found in the hearts of mankind in all walks of life. We need to work on a better screening method to help identify those who are mentally ill and those who are biased before they get access to guns or weapons of any type. We need more mental institutions and professional doctors to develop things to help with the working of the mind of people.

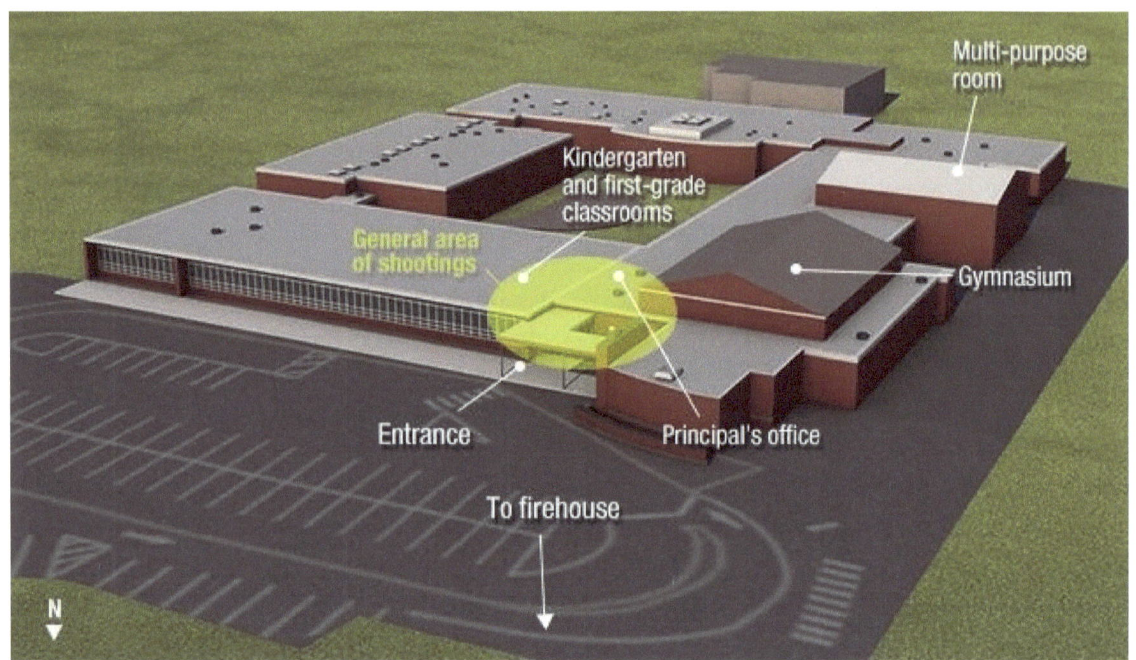

Sandy Hook

Twenty-six people -- 20 students and six adults were shot and killed at the Sandy Hook Elementary School in Newtown, Connecticut on December 14, 2012.

At the police station, dispatchers began to take calls from inside the school. Authorities say the first emergency call about the shooting came in at "approximately" 9:30 a.m.

"Sandy Hook school caller is indicating she thinks someone is shooting in the building," a dispatcher told fire and medical personnel, according to 911 tapes.

The first officer arrived on the scene of the Sandy Hook school shooting two minutes and 41 seconds after the first police radio broadcast of the shooting. Previous CNN reporting cited an incorrect arrival time based on earlier reports.

Police reported that no law enforcement officers discharged their weapons at any point.

"The gunman took his own life," police said. "He took out a handgun and shot himself in a classroom as law enforcement officers approached," officials said.

Twenty students, ages 6 and 7, and six adults were killed at the school.

Police secured the building, ensuring no other shooters were on site. Police then escorted students and faculty out of the building to a nearby firehouse.

As reports of the shooting made their way around town, frantic parents descended on the firehouse where the children had been taken.

By nightfall, the firehouse became a gathering point for parents and family members whose loved ones would never walk out of the school.

Source CNN

This is undoubtedly one of the worst events in modern history that involved so many children in our society. The parents then came forward and tried to lobby the politicians to change the gun laws and protect the children from any more of these types of incidents ever happening again. We are a modern-day society with backwards thinking. The fact is that knowledge without wisdom caused more catastrophes like this one because nothing changed.

The Bath School Disaster of 1927 – 45 Victims

It was a real tragedy that happened in 1927 in a little town in Michigan. Many children were killed because of the fact a mad man set off bombs that injured 58 people and killed 45 victims.

2007 – 33 Victims at Virginia Tech

A lone gunman killed 33 people, including himself, on the campus of Virginia Polytechnic Institute and State University in Blacksburg, Virginia, on April 16, 2007. It is considered the deadliest shooting incident by a single gunman in United States history.

University of Texas Massacre – 1966 – 16 Victims

On August 1, 1966, a former marine and engineering student took a sniper rifle to the top of a tower on the campus of University of Texas-Austin and started shooting people as they walked by. The shooter, targeting people at random, killed 16 people during his 96-minute rampage before he was shot and killed by police officers.

Columbine – 1999 – 15 Victims

Columbine is probably the most famous school shooting in American history. It's been the subject of a Hollywood film and a popular documentary. The shooting at Columbine High School in Littleton, Colorado, occurred on April 20, 1999. Two shooters walked into the school armed with guns and homemade bombs and killed 12 students and a teacher. They both committed suicide at the end of their rampage.

Chapter 9 - Synopsis

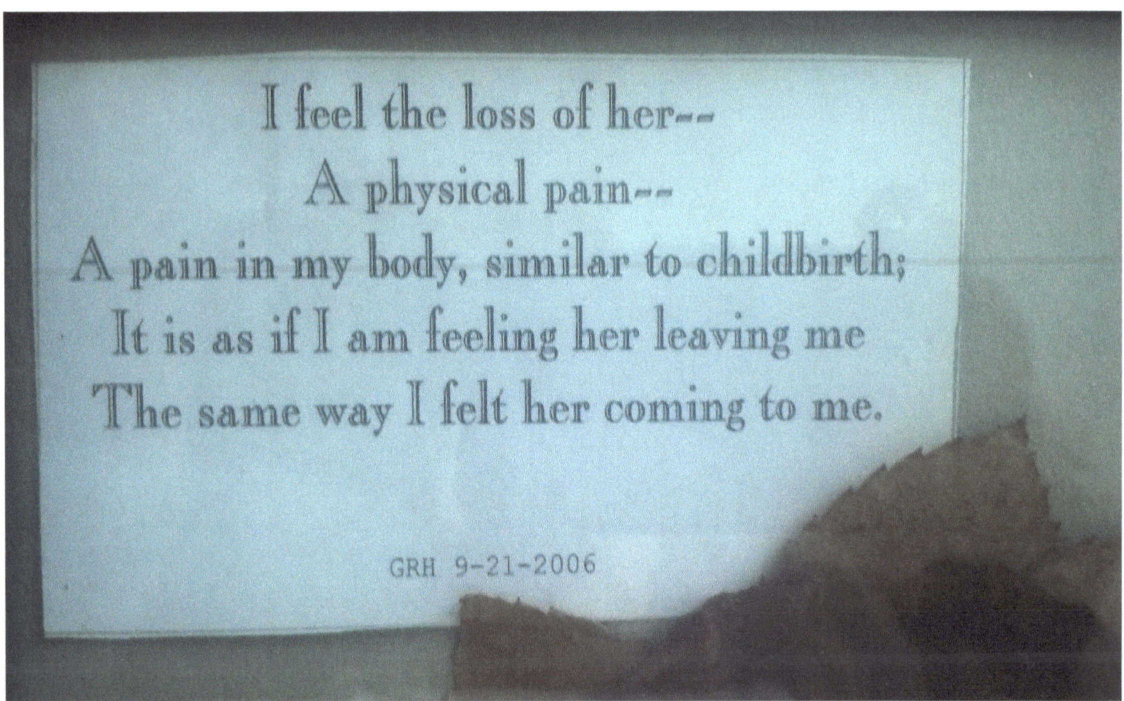

How many parents will need to face this bitter pill?

There are many other school shootings, and no doubt before my book is published, there might even be another shooting. I do pray not, but until we as Americans stand up and do something about it this will not stop. Don't be fooled by the gun lobbyists' claim that it is not guns that kill but people. It is the gun in the wrong hands that is doing the killing. If the guns were not so readily available, then the wrong people would not have access to them. We need to work on the instrument of death to keep it out of the hands of those who would use them to kill others.

All those beautiful people have died in vain if we let those who fight for the right to carry a gun without any restrictions win. A hunter or marksman know well that the gun poses danger to individuals or groups if not handled properly and in the right hands. It is time that we act, and not let the power of the dollar win out. Lobbyist often fight for the NRA, but where are the lobbyist for the dead who were shot and killed senselessly with a gun? It is time that we form our own group and get financial backing and change the laws of the land.

I have raised children and I have had a hand in helping my friends with their children at times, and I cannot imagine the pain that these parents are suffering right now. I also don't want to hear about future parents who bring children into the world and lose them so senselessly. There are steps that can be taken and should be applied immediately. No need to hesitate! The death of one more child is not necessary. Every Congressperson who votes against gun restrictions should be put to the test and must go and sit with the parents who have lost their child. Explain to that parent why it is important to leave our gun laws so open that anyone can access a gun.

The gun toting individual who is responsible should not mind background checks across state lines, and restrictions on the number of guns and the types of guns that they have in their possession. Minor children should not have ownership of guns. If the parent wants them to learn how to hunt, then let the parent buy the gun and be held accountable. These are just a few of the things that could prevent such tragedies. When new law enforcement individuals come to the office, do not only train them at an academy but let them also have a psychological evaluation. The evaluations should be held yearly no matter how long they are in office. Act on the results!

Guns across America!

Need not be murder across America!

Contact your representative

Voice your opinion

ISBN: 13: 978-1986356220

ISBN: 10: 1986356221

www.ingramcontent.com/pod-product-compliance
Lightning Source LLC
Chambersburg PA
CBHW040035240726
48664CB00003B/940